DISCOVERING AMERICA

Lower Atlantic

NORTH CAROLINA • SOUTH CAROLINA

By
Thomas G. Aylesworth
Virginia L. Aylesworth

CHELSEA HOUSE PUBLISHERS
New York • Philadelphia

3   5   7   9   8   6   4

Library of Congress Cataloging-in-Publication Data

Aylesworth, Thomas G.
    Lower Atlantic: North Carolina, South Carolina
Thomas G. Aylesworth, Virginia L. Aylesworth.
        p. cm.—(Discovering America)
    Includes bibliographical references and index.
    ISBN 0-7910-3401-1.
            0-7910-3419-4 (pbk.)
    1. South Atlantic States—Juvenile literature. 2. North Carolina—Juvenile literature. 3. South
Carolina—Juvenile literature. I. Aylesworth, Virginia L. II. Title. III. Series: Aylesworth,
Thomas G. Discovering America.

F209.3.A943   1995   94-40429
917.56—dc20   CIP

CONTENTS

SOUTH CAROLINA 45

North Carolina

The great seal of the state of North Carolina was first designed in 1893 and has since been modified. As it exists today, it contains a drawing of two female figures in the center of a circle. On the left stands Liberty, holding in her right hand a scroll inscribed with the word "Constitution." In her left hand is a staff with a cap on it. On the right is seated Plenty, holding out three heads of grain toward Liberty in her right hand, with the end of a horn of plenty in her left hand. Behind the figures are mountains and an ocean, and in the ocean is a three-masted ship to the right of Plenty. Above the figures is the date May 20, 1775, representing the signing of the Mecklenburg Declaration of Independence, a set of anti-British resolutions written up by the citizens of Mecklenburg County in North Carolina. Surrounding the figures is a larger circle, with The Great Seal of the State of North Carolina around it, and at the bottom of this circle is the state motto, *Esse Quam Videri* ("To be rather than to seem").

State Flag

In 1885, North Carolina adopted its flag. On the left is a blue vertical stripe. In the center are enscribed N and C, with a star in between. Above the inscription is a banner with the date May 20, 1775, and below there is another banner with the date April 12, 1776. These two dates are the dates of the North Carolina declarations of independence, which were made before the national Declaration of Independence. To the right of the blue stripe are two horizontal stripes—red on the top and white on the bottom.

Called Woods's River until 1750, the scenic New River was renamed for a ferry captain.

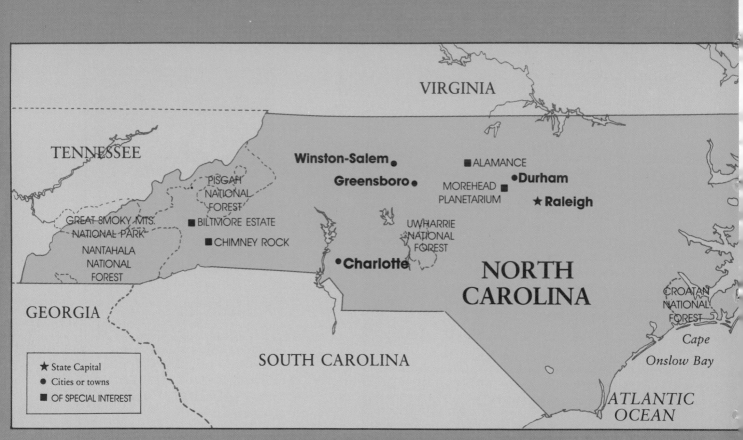

VIRGINIA

TENNESSEE

Winston-Salem ●
■ ALAMANCE
Greensboro ●
MOREHEAD ■ ● Durham
PLANETARIUM
★ Raleigh

PISGAH
NATIONAL
FOREST

GREAT SMOKY MTS.
NATIONAL PARK
■ BILTMORE ESTATE
■ CHIMNEY ROCK

NANTAHALA
NATIONAL
FOREST

● Charlotte

UWHARRIE
NATIONAL
FOREST

NORTH
CAROLINA

GEORGIA

CROATAN
NATIONAL
FOREST

Cape

Onslow Bay

SOUTH CAROLINA

ATLANTIC
OCEAN

★ State Capital
● Cities or towns
■ OF SPECIAL INTEREST

0 10 20   40   60   80   100   120   140   160   180   200   Miles
0 10 20 40 60 80 100 120 140 160 180 200 220 240 260 280 300 325 Kilometres

State Motto: *Esse Quam Videri* (To Be Rather Than to Seem)

State Tree: Loblolly Pine

Nicknames: Tar Heel State, Old North State

State Song: "The Old North State"

Size: 52,669 square miles (28th largest)
Population: 6,842,691 (10th largest)

NORTH CAROLINA
At a Glance

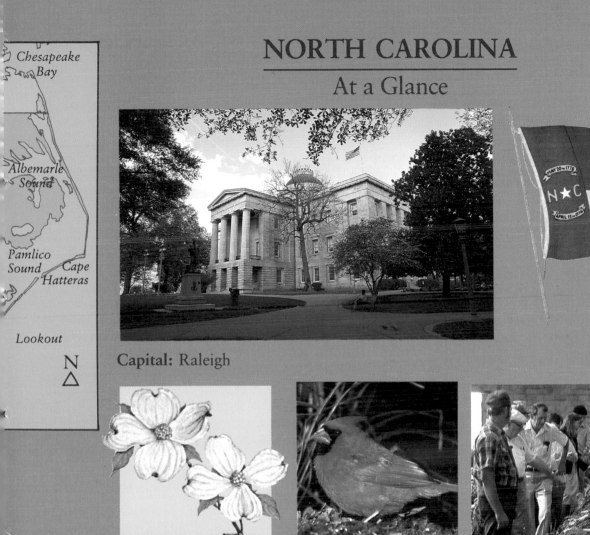

Capital: Raleigh

State Flower:
Flowering Dogwood

State Bird: Cardinal

Major Industries: Textiles, tobacco products, furniture,
agriculture

Major Crops: Tobacco, soybeans, truck crops, corn, peanuts

Chesapeake Bay

Albemarle Sound

Pamlico Sound

Cape Hatteras

Lookout

N

State Name and Nicknames

Both North and South Carolina were once a single territory called Carolina, originally named after King Charles I of France and later to honor Kings Charles I and Charles II of England. The Latin version of Charles is *Carolus*. Carolinus is an adjective form of the name, and Carolina is the feminine form of the adjective.

One of the nicknames of North Carolina is the *Old North State,* because it was separated from South Carolina in 1729. Another name is the *Turpentine State,* after one of its principal agricultural products. The most common nickname, however, is the *Tar Heel State.* The origin of this is debated. One story suggests the name was given to North Carolina soldiers in the Civil War by some troops from Mississippi. The North Carolinians were chased by Union troops from a hill that they were occupying, and the Mississippians said that they had forgotten to "tar their heels" and could not keep their position. Another tale says that North Carolinians had remained to defend their position and offered to "tar the heels" of the regiment that had fled.

State Motto

Esse Quam Videri

The Latin motto, which means "To be rather than to seem," was adopted in 1893. It comes from the writings of the Roman statesman, scholar, and orator Marcus Tullius Cicero.

State Capital

New Bern was the capital of North Carolina from 1770 to 1776, and there was no fixed capital from 1776 to 1794. Raleigh was selected as the capital in 1792, but it was not used until 1794.

State Flower

The flowering dogwood, *Cornus florida,* was made the state flower of North Carolina by the state legislature in 1941.

State Gemstone

Emerald

State Shell

Scotch bonnet

State Tree

Pinus palustris, the southern pine, was named the state tree of North Carolina in 1963.

State Bird

Cardinalis cardinalis, the cardinal, was adopted as the state bird by the legislature in 1943.

State Colors

Red and blue were chosen in 1945.

State Fish

The channel bass, *Sciaeops ocellatus,* was chosen state fish in 1971.

State Insect

The honeybee, *Apis mellifera,* was adopted as the state insect in 1973.

State Mammal

Sciurus carolinensis, the gray squirrel, was named the state mammal in 1969.

State Reptile

The eastern box turtle, genus *Terrapene*, was selected as state reptile in 1979.

State Toast

The Tar Heel Toast to North Carolina was adopted as the official toast in 1957.

State Song

"The Old North State" was adopted as the official state song in 1927. The lyrics were written by William Gaston, with music by Mrs. E. E. Randolph.

Population

The population of North Carolina in 1992 was 6,842,691, making it the tenth most populous state. There are 140.5 persons per square mile. About 99 percent of the population lives in cities and towns. Almost 99 percent of North Carolinians were born

Mount Mitchell was named for Professor Elisha Mitchell, who fell to his death while trying to verify his earlier measurement of the mountain's altitude.

in the United States. Most of those from other countries came from England, France, or other European nations.

Industries

The principal industries of North Carolina are agriculture, tobacco, and tourism. In 1991 tourism earned $7 billion in North Carolina. With 27.3 percent of North Carolinians employed in manufacturing, the state has the highest percentage of people employed in that sector in the country. The chief products manufactured are textiles, tobacco products, electrical and electronic equipment, chemicals, furniture, food products, and nonelectrical machinery.

Agriculture

The chief crops of the state are tobacco, soybeans, corn, peanuts, sweet potatoes, feed grains, vegetables, and fruits. North Carolina is also a livestock state; there are estimated to be some 950,000 head of cattle, 3.6 million hogs and pigs, and 19.3 million chickens on its farms. Yellow pine, oak, hickory, poplar, and maple trees are harvested for timber. Crushed stone, sand, gravel, and feldspar are important mineral products. In 1992 commercial fishing earned $57.5 million.

North Carolina's tobacco fields produce a crop worth about one billion dollars a year.

Government

The governor and lieutenant governor of North Carolina serve four-year terms. Other state officers elected to four-year terms are the secretary of state, attorney general, auditor, treasurer, superintendent of public instruction, and the commissioners of agriculture, insurance, and labor. The state legislature consists of a 50-member senate and a 120-member house of representatives, all of whom serve two-year terms. The senators are elected from districts divided according to population, as are the representatives. Each of the 100 counties in North Carolina has at least one representative. The most recent state constitution was adopted in 1868 and amended in 1875. In addition to its two U.S. senators, North Carolina has 12 representatives in the U.S. House of Representatives. The state has 14 votes in the electoral college.

Sports

Sporting events on the college and secondary school levels are held all over the state. On the college level, the NCAA basketball championship was won by Wake Forest in 1955, by North Carolina State in 1974 and 1983, by the University of North Carolina in 1982 and 1993, and by Duke University in 1991 and 1992. In football, Duke won the Sugar Bowl in 1945, the Orange Bowl in

A view of the Charlotte skyline.

1955, and the Cotton Bowl in 1961; Wake Forest won the Independence Bowl in 1992; and North Carolina won the Peach Bowl in 1993.

In professional sports, the Charlotte Hornets of the National Basketball Association play in the Charlotte Coliseum.

Major Cities

Charlotte (population 395,934). Settled in 1748, this is North Carolina's most populous city. Early in its history, the city became a regional retail, financial, and distribution center and at one time was the country's leader in the textile industry. During the Revolutionary War, British general Lord Cornwallis occupied the city for a while, but the citizens resisted him so much that he called the community a "hornet's nest." This epithet is carried proudly on the city seal. In 1799, gold was discovered here, and the area

Discovery Place is a hands-on children's museum in Charlotte; it's focus is on the sciences.

became the major gold producer in the United States until the California Gold Rush in 1848.

Places to visit in Charlotte: the Mint Museum, the Hezekiah Alexander Homesite History Museum, the Nature Museum, Discovery Place, the Latta Plantation Park, the Spirit Square Center for the Arts, Carowinds Theme Park, and the James K. Polk Memorial State Historic Site.

Greensboro (population 183,894). Founded in 1808, this is a diversified industrial city whose products are textiles, cigarettes, machinery, and electronic components. The town was settled by the Quakers, Germans, Scottish, and Irish, who gave it its enthusiasm for political, religious, and economic freedom.

Places to visit in Greensboro: the Weatherspoon Art Gallery, the Greensboro Historical Museum, the Guilford Courthouse National Military Park, the Natural Science Center of

Greensboro, and Hagan-Stone Park.

Raleigh (population 212,050). Founded in 1792, the state capital is a commercial, educational, and retail center. Named for Sir Walter Raleigh, the town itself was laid out in 1792 following a resolution by the general assembly that an "unalterable seat of government" be established within ten miles of Isaac Hunter's tavern. (Actually, the planners found a site within four miles of the tavern.)

Places to visit in Raleigh: the State Capitol Building, the State Legislative Building, the North Carolina Museum of Natural Sciences, the North Carolina Museum of History, the North Carolina Museum of Art, the Mordecai Historical Park and Mordecai House (1785 and 1826), the Oakwood District, William B. Umstead State Park, Falls Lake State Recreation Area, and the Greencroft Botanical Gardens.

Places to Visit
The National Park Service

The Mint Museum of Art is housed in the reconstructed U.S. Mint.

The Biltmore Estate in Asheville was built in 1895 for George Vanderbilt. The 17 acres of gardens were landscaped by Frederick Law Olmsted.

maintains 13 areas in the state of North Carolina: Cape Hatteras National Seashore, Fort Raleigh National Historic Site, Great Smoky Mountains National Park, Carl Sandburg Home National Historic Site, Guilford Courthouse National Military Park, Moores Creek National Battlefield, Wright Brothers National Memorial, part of the Blue Ridge Parkway, Cape Lookout National Seashore, Croatan National Forest, Nantahala National Forest, Pisgah National Forest, and Uwharrie National Forest. In addition, there are 31 state recreation areas.

Asheboro: North Carolina Zoological Park. Eight hundred African animals are displayed in six outdoor natural habitats.

Asheville: Biltmore Estate. Formal gardens grace the grounds of this 250-room chateau-style house, built between 1890 and 1895.

Bath State Historic Site: This marks the oldest incorporated town in the state and contains

The USS North Carolina, docked in Wilmington, has been open to the public since 1961. It serves as a memorial to World War II veterans.

several historical buildings.

Chapel Hill: North Carolina Botanical Garden. A variety of trees and plants of the southeastern United States are grown in the garden, which features wild flower areas and herbs.

Cherokee: Oconaluftee Indian Village. This replica of an Indian village of 250 years ago includes a seven-sided council house.

Concord: Reed Gold Mine State Historic Site. It was here that the first gold strike in the United States occurred—mine tours and a panning area are featured.

Durham: Duke Chapel at Duke University. A beautiful Gothic-style chapel, with a carillon of 50 bells in a 210-foot tower rises over the campus.

Edenton: Historic Edenton. A tour may be taken of historic properties, including the Cupola House (1725) and the James Iredell House (1773).

Greenville: Village of Yesteryear. A restoration of old time Greenville preserves the heritage of this agricultural community.

High Point: Peterson Doll and Miniature Museum. Some of the more than 1,000 dolls here date back to the 15th century.

Manteo: Elizabeth II State Historic Site. A reproduction of a sixteenth-century sailing ship that brought the first English colonists to the New World over 400 years ago.

Mount Gilead: Town Creek Indian Mound State Historic Site. This reconstruction of a

Visitors to the Reed Gold Mine can walk the mining trails, as well as a restored section of the underground shaft.

sixteenth-century Indian ceremonial center includes the stockade, temples, and mortuary.

New Bern: Tryon Palace and Gardens. The one-time royal governor's mansion, built in 1767 and burned in 1798, was restored in the 20th century.

Reidsville: Chinqua-Penn Plantation. This English country house has extensive formal and rose gardens.

Salisbury: Dr. Josephus Hall House. Built in 1820, this large antebellum house is surrounded by giant oaks and century-old boxwoods.

Wilmington: USS North Carolina Battleship Memorial. The World War II battleship can be toured.

Winston-Salem: Old Salem. Here is a reconstruction of a planned community settled in the 1700s by the Moravians, a German Protestant group.

Events

There are many events and organizations that schedule activities of various kinds in the state of North Carolina. Here are some of them.

Sports: Central Tarheel Balloon Race (Burlington); Lumberjack Day (Burnsville); Easter Egg Fighters (Cherryville); Sailing Regatta (Elizabeth City); Greater Greensboro Open Golf Tournament (Greensboro); Governor's Cup Regatta (Henderson); auto racing (Hickory); Gas Boat Drag Championships (High Point); Planters Pat Bradley International Golf Tournament (High Point); Big Rock Blue Marlin Tournament (Morehead City); Annual Hang Gliding Spectacular (Nags Head); Rogallo Kite Festival (Nags Head); PGA/World Golf Hall of Fame Pro-Am Golf Tournament (Pinehurst); Stoneybrook Steeplechase Races (Southern Pines); Southport-Oak Island Masters Putting Tournament (Southport); Tarheel Classic Horse Show (Statesville); Tanglewood Park Steeplechase (Winston-Salem).

Arts and Crafts: Southern Highland Handicraft Guild Fair (Asheville); Mt. Mitchell Crafts Festival (Burnsville); CenterFest (Durham); Riverspree (Elizabeth City); Albemarle Craftsman's Fair (Elizabeth City); Mistletoe Show (Elizabeth City); Dogwood Festival (Fayetteville); Macon County Gemboree (Franklin); Grandfather Mountain Nature Photography Weekend (Linville); Carolina Dogwood Festival (Statesville); North Carolina Azalea Festival (Wilmington); Riverfest (Wilmington); Piedmont Crafts Fair (Winston-Salem).

Music: Shindig on the Green (Asheville); Mountain Dance and Folk Festival (Asheville); An Appalachian Summer (Boone); Festival of the Arts (Brevard); Summer Festival of Music (Brevard); Music in the Mountains (Burnsville); Charlotte Symphony (Charlotte); American Dance Festival (Durham); Greensboro Symphony (Greensboro); Old Time Fiddlers' Convention (Jefferson); "Singing on the Mountain" (Linville); International Folk Festival (Fayetteville); North Carolina Symphony (Raleigh); National Whistlers' Convention (Raleigh); ArtsPlosure (Raleigh); Folk Festival (Raleigh); North Carolina Dance Theater (Winston-Salem); Winston-Salem Symphony (Winston-Salem).

Entertainment: Fall Festival (Asheboro); Gee Haw Whimmy Diddle World Competition (Asheville); Springfest (Charlotte); Festival in the Park (Charlotte); Shooting in the New Year (Cherryville); Festival of Festivals (Franklin); Macon County Fair (Franklin); Leaflookers Clogging Jamboree (Franklin); North Carolina Apple Festival (Hendersonville); Grandfather

Mountain Highland Games (Linville); Atlantic Beach Mackerel Tournament (Morehead City); Waldensian Celebration of the Glorious Return (Morganton); State Fair (Raleigh); Iredell County Fair (Statesville); Washington Summer Festival (Washington); Carolina Street Scene Festival (Winston-Salem); Dixie Classic Fair (Winston-Salem).

Tours: Old Homes Tour (Beaufort); Tour of Homes (Blowing Rock); Edenton Pilgrimage (Edenton); House and Garden Tour (Southern Pines).

Theater: Shakespeare in the Park (Asheville); "Horn in the West" (Boone); Parkway Playhouse (Burnsville); "Unto These Hills" (Cherokee); North Carolina Shakespeare Festival (High Point); "Strike at the Wind" (Pembroke); "The Lost Colony" (Manteo); "From This Day Forward" (Valdese); "The Immortal Showboat" (Wilmington).

Folkmoot USA is the largest festival of its kind in the United States. More than 300 dancers from around the world gather here to perform in native costumes.

The Eno River near Durham. The central region of North Carolina is characterized mostly by low-lying marshland, shallow lakes, and rivers.

The Land and the Climate

North Carolina is a true cross-section of America, with its mountains, plains, and coastline. The state has three main land regions—the Atlantic Coastal Plain, the Piedmont, and the Blue Ridge.

The Atlantic Coastal Plain is part of the long coastal plain that extends from New York to southern Florida. Eastern North Carolina, along the Atlantic Ocean, looks something like a giant foot, the heel consisting of a chain of slender land ridges extending several miles out to sea. The region includes swamps, prairies, and rich farmland. The Outer Banks consist of sand dunes, reefs, sand bars, and islands off the shoreline of the state. Many of them have colorful names, such as Cape Fear, Cape Hatteras, Cape Lookout, and Nags Head. They are dangerous to mariners, especially those who don't know the treacherous currents of these waters.

The Cape Hatteras Lighthouse is the tallest in the United States. It sends warning signals to ships sailing in the treacherous waters of the Atlantic Ocean near Raleigh Bay and Pamlico Sound.

The Atlantic Coastal Plain extends from the shoreline to the rocky, hilly areas in the central part of the state. At its eastern edge, the area is one of low, level marshland, covered by trees and water. There are many swamps, shallow lakes, and rivers overhung by cypress trees draped with Spanish moss. One of the nation's largest swamps, the Dismal Swamp, is located in the northeast area of this region. Tree-less, grassy prairies called *savannas* are another feature of the coastal plain. The western section of the coastal plain has rich farmland; and is referred to as "Tobaccoland." In its southern part are many sand hills, where such popular winter resorts as Pinehurst and Southern Pines are located. In the northern coastal plain there are many peanut farms.

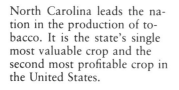

North Carolina leads the nation in the production of tobacco. It is the state's single most valuable crop and the second most profitable crop in the United States.

Grandfather Mountain is the highest mountain in the Blue Ridge chain. It lies between the Smoky Mountains, to the west, and the Piedmont Range, to the east.

   The Piedmont is an extension of a strip of land that runs from Delaware to Alabama at the foot of the mountains. This region in the central part of North Carolina is said to look like the face of an elderly man, whose brow, nose, and jaw point to the west. Its high ground rises to about 1,500 feet before it reaches the mountains. Here most of the state's manufacturing takes place, and cotton is an important crop. The Piedmont has more people than the other two regions.

   The **Blue Ridge** is the mountainous area of North Carolina, along the western border. The Blue Ridge Mountains stretch from southern Pennsylvania to northern Georgia; in North Carolina the Blue Ridge includes other ranges as well—the Bald, Black, Brushy, Great Smoky, Iron, South, Stone, and Unaka Ranges. All of them taken together form a part of the Appalachian Mountains. Some mountains near the Blue Ridge are more than a mile above sea level, including Mount Mitchell, the highest mountain east of the Mississippi River, rising to a height of 6,684 feet. The mountains are covered with forests and the valleys contain good farm land and grazing for dairy cattle. Great Smoky Mountains National Park and the Blue Ridge Parkway are major scenic attractions in this region.

The mountainous areas of the Blue Ridge and the Piedmont are where many of the state's rivers originate. Their waters flow from altitudes that are often more than a mile above sea level, creating white-water rapids that are ideal for rafting and canoeing.

Most of North Carolina's rivers start in the Blue Ridge or in the Piedmont, flowing down the slopes of the mountains toward the coastal plain. They tumble over waterfalls and form fast-moving rapids, until they hit the estuaries, or river mouths, near the coast. Many of these waterfalls and rapids are used in the production of electric power. Important rivers of the state include the Roanoke, the Neuse, the Tar, and the Cape Fear. North Carolina's largest dams are in the western section on the Hiwassee, the Little Tennessee, and the Nanta-

hala Rivers. The only natural lakes in the state are on the Atlantic Coastal Plain, the largest being Lake Mattamuskeet, which is about fifteen miles long and six miles wide.

Temperatures in North Carolina range from 67 to 88 degrees Fahrenheit in July to 31 to 51 degrees F. in January; the warmer temperatures are usually found along the coast. The state has moderate rainfall, averaging around 44 inches yearly. During the present century, there has been an average of one hurricane a year.

The Uwharrie National Forest in the Blue Ridge Mountains includes many areas that are among the state's most popular campsites.

The History

A ceremonial mask made by the Cherokee Indians of North Carolina. Predominantly farmers who grew maize (corn), beans, squash, and gourds, the Cherokee were the largest tribe in southeastern North America and spoke a language related to that of the Iroquois.

The first white man to explore the land that was to become North Carolina was probably Giovanni da Verrazano, an Italian sailor who was conducting an expedition for King Francis I of France in 1524. He visited the Cape Fear area and gave a glowing report of what he saw to the king, but he was not interested in setting up a colony there.

In 1526 Lucas Vásquez de Ayllón of Spain did establish a colony near Cape Fear, but disease and starvation led to the end of that experiment. Another Spaniard, Hernando de Soto, led his expedition over the mountains in the southwestern corner of the territory in 1540. Heading west, de Soto was looking for gold, but he found the Mississippi River instead.

At that time there were about 35,000 Indians in the region, belonging to some 30 tribes. The five most numerous and important tribes were the Cherokee, who lived in the mountains of the west; the Hatteras, along the coast; and the Catawba, Chowanoc, and Tuscarora in the coastal plain and the Piedmont.

The first Englishmen came to the territory in 1585, when Sir Walter Raleigh sent an expedition to settle on Roanoke Island. It became the first English colony in America. But once again, life in the New World wilderness was too difficult, and the settlers were forced to return to England in 1586.

Then one of American history's most puzzling mysteries occurred. Raleigh sent another expedition to Roanoke Island in 1587, appointing John White as governor of the settlement. White established the colony and sailed back to England for supplies. Queen Elizabeth I kept him in England for a time, and when he returned to the colony in 1590, there was no one left. Only the word "Croatoan," crudely scratched on a tree, remained as a clue to the colony's fate: it may have referred to the Croatan Indians, and there was speculation that a

The Spanish explorer Hernando de Soto led a band of 600 soldiers through present-day Georgia and the Carolinas after landing in Florida in 1539. As governor of Cuba, he had heard of great wealth in Florida and came to the region in search of gold and silver. Though he never found the treasures he sought, and much of his wandering through southeastern North America was plagued by Indian attacks and disease, de Soto and his men are credited with discovering the Mississippi River in 1541.

massacre had taken place. Even today, however, no one knows what happened to the more than 100 men, women, and children of Roanoke Island. Among the missing was the first child born of English parents in America—Virginia Dare. The settlement became known as the Lost Colony.

King Charles I of England gave his attorney general, Sir Robert Heath, part of the English claim in the Americas in 1629. This included not only what would become both North and South Carolina, but all the land west of them to the other side of the continent. The region was named the Province of Carolana, from the Latin word *Carolus,* for Charles. But Heath decided not to try to settle the area.

People from Virginia were the first to become permanent settlers in the Province of Carolana. They came in about 1650 and built their homes in the Albemarle Sound region. In 1663 King Charles II of England deeded the province to eight of his friends, making them lords, proprietors, or ruling noblemen, of the colony. These men divided the territory into three counties: Albemarle, in the north; Clarendon, in the Cape Fear region; and Craven, in what is now South Carolina. Formal English rule came to North Carolina in 1664, when William Drummond was appointed Governor of Albemarle County; that county had the only government in the North Carolina region after Clarendon County was abolished in 1667.

Some of the residents of Albemarle County took over from the governor in 1678, because they suspected that he was more interested in making money than in governing in the best interest of the community. This group controlled the county for a year and installed John Culpeper as governor. The revolt became known as Culpeper's Rebellion. In fact, it was only one of several uprisings against outside rule. Between 1664 and 1689, the colonists drove five Albemarle governors from office. As a result, more competent governors were appointed to rule the entire Carolina colony in 1689, with North and South Carolina having separate deputy governors. In 1711 the two areas became separate colonies.

Each year a historical reenactment entitled *The Lost Colony* is presented on Roanoke Island. It dramatizes the story of the second Roanoke colony, established by the English in 1587, which had completely vanished by the time John White returned to the island in 1590. To this day, the mystery of the colony's disappearance cannot be fully explained.

Settlers continued to come into North Carolina, and in 1705 the colony incorporated its first town—Bath—near the mouth of the Pamlico River. In 1710 Swiss and German settlers founded New Bern on the Neuse River in Tuscarora Indian territory. On September 22, 1711, the community was raided by the Tuscarora, who resented the seizure of their land. Within two hours of the attack, the settlement was in ruins. Hundreds had been massacred and their buildings and crops put to the torch. This was the beginning of the Tuscarora War, which went on for 18 months before the Indians were defeated.

Meanwhile, on the coast, colonists were being terrorized by pirates, who preyed on merchant vessels, supply ships, and other maritime

This sailing vessel, anchored in Manteo Harbor, is similar to British ships that crossed the Atlantic on voyages of exploration during the reign of Queen Elizabeth I.

traffic. It was not until 1718 that the pirates were defeated near Ocracoke Island—in a battle that resulted in the death of the famous pirate Blackbeard (Edward Teach).

The lords proprietors sold their land back to the British Crown in 1729, and North Carolina became a royal colony. Fortunately, the king sent good governors to administer the affairs of the colony, and it prospered under their leadership. The population grew from 36,000 in 1729 to 350,000 by 1775.

North Carolina contributed both money and soldiers to the British cause in several wars. The unusually named War of Jenkins' Ear (1739–44) was fought against the Spaniards in Georgia. It was so called because it was alleged that Thomas Jenkins, an English seaman, had been attacked by Spanish sailors who cut off his ear. Queen Anne's War (1702–13), King George's War (1744–48), and the French and Indian War (1754–63) were other conflicts in which North Carolina took an active part. Troops under the command of Hugh Waddell of Wilmington defeated the Cherokee Indians in 1760 in a battle at Fort Dobbs, near present-day Statesville.

The 1770s brought oppressive English taxes upon the colonies. Although they were levied to help pay for the colonial wars, the colonists were angry, and a group of North Carolinians called the Sons of Liberty demonstrated against the taxes and even led an armed rebellion. In the western part of the colony, an organization of farmers called the Regulators also rebelled. The colony's governor, William Tryon, used more than 1,000 soldiers to break up the Regulators in the Battle of Alamance in 1771.

There was a North Carolina delegation to the First Continental Congress in Philadelphia in 1774. When the Revolutionary War began in 1775, North Carolinians were divided. On the one hand there were the Whigs, who opposed the English; on the other were the Tories, who were loyal to the Crown. On February 27, 1776, Whig troops led by Colonels Richard Caswell and Alexander Lillington beat the Tories in the Battle of Moore's Creek Bridge—the first Revolutionary War battle in the colony.

North Carolina was the first American colony to instruct its delegation to the Continental Congress to vote for independence (April 12, 1776). A constitution was adopted by the colony that year, and on July 21, 1778, North Carolina approved the Articles of Confederation, which united the 13 original colonies under a national government.

Few battles were fought in North Carolina during the War for Independence, but state troops fought the British in Virginia, Georgia, and South Carolina. Then, in 1781, British general Lord Charles Cornwallis moved his troops into North Carolina. Though he defeated American General Nathanael Greene at the Battle of Guilford Courthouse on March 15, 1781, British casualties were nearly twice those of the Americans. Greatly weakened by this battle, Cornwallis's army was forced to abandon most of the Carolina area.

North Carolina was slow in approving the new United States Constitution, because it favored states' rights over a strong central government. Many improvements suggested by North Carolina were incorporated into the Bill of Rights—the first 10 amendments to the Constitution.

Fort Macon, located between Morehead City and Beaufort at the northern tip of Onslow Bay, was completed in 1834. It was a stronghold for the Confederate Army during the Civil War.

A portrait of Revolutionary War general Nathanael Greene. After George Washington chose him to succeed General Horatio Gates as Commander of the Southern army, Greene fought fiercely against the British in the battles of Guilford Courthouse, Hobkirk's Hill, and Eutaw Springs. Under Greene's command, American troops in the Carolinas inflicted heavy losses on the British, which eventually led to Cornwallis's surrender at Yorktown in October 1781.

From about 1800 to 1835, North Carolina's development was so slow—in commerce, industry, and transportation—that it was nicknamed the Rip Van Winkle State. Then came revision of the state constitution in 1835, which gave most taxpaying men the right to vote. This meant that residents of the sparsely populated western part of the state had more representation and thus more incentive to develop their area. New public schools, railroads, and roads were built. Agriculture increased and manufacturing began to appear.

At the beginning of the Civil War, North Carolina tried to preserve the Union: it was one of the last southern states to join the Confederate States of America in 1861. Much of eastern North Carolina was captured early in the war, but the port of Wilmington was open to Confederate supply ships until 1865. More than 10 battles were fought in the state, of which the costliest in human life was at Benton-

ville on March 19–21, 1865. Union troops under the command of General William T. Sherman defeated the Confederate forces of General Joseph E. Johnston. North Carolina sent 125,000 men to serve in the Confederate Armies; approximately one fourth of all Confederate soldiers killed were from the state.

After the war ended in 1865, North Carolina was under the rule of the Federal Army during the Reconstruction period (to 1877). A new state constitution was drawn up in 1868 by Republicans hostile to the defeated South. Slavery was outlawed and blacks were given the right to vote—often strongly influenced by Northerners who had come south to profit from the postwar confusion and distress. These people (the carpetbaggers, as they were called for the fabric satchels in which they carried their belongings) fostered hostility between Democrats and Republicans, blacks and whites.

Kitty Hawk was the site of the first successful motor-powered airplane flights made on December 17, 1903, by Orville and Wilbur Wright. After many mechanical breakdowns and delays caused by blustery weather, the Wright brothers completed two flights each, the longest flight lasting 59 seconds and covering 852 feet against a 20-mile wind. In the years that followed, the Wrights, who owned a bicycle shop in Dayton, Ohio, improved their designs, increased the horsepower of the engines they used, and perfected many early techniques of flight. They were the first to teach Army personnel to fly and are considered two of the greatest pioneers in aviation history.

One result of the abolition of slavery was that it became almost impossible to maintain large plantations. Without free labor, the large farms had to be split up, especially those growing labor-intensive crops like tobacco and cotton. The number of farms in North Carolina rose from about 75,000 in 1860 to almost 150,000 in 1880. By the late 1800s, farm production had recovered to its prewar level. Industry was also on the rise, especially the tobacco industry and furniture manufacturing.

In the early twentieth century, North Carolina's state government began to improve schools and roads. It developed one of the best state universities in the nation. Highway construction was so extensive that by the 1920s, the state was re-nicknamed the Good Roads State. The Wright Brothers had made their first airplane flight at Kitty Hawk on December 17, 1903, opening the door into the new age of aviation.

During the Great Depression of the 1930s, many North Carolina farmers went bankrupt, and businesses and factories were forced to close. Then the state government lowered local taxes and took control of all highways and public schools, while the federal government regulated agricultural production. Gradually farm prices and incomes began to rise. Welfare laws were passed, teachers' salaries were raised, and the working hours of factory laborers were reduced.

During World War II (1941–45), more than 2,000,000 servicemen were trained in North Carolina. The mills that handled cotton products supplied the armed forces with more textiles than any other state. By this time the state also led the nation in the production of tobacco products and wooden furniture.

After the war, North Carolina began to improve its health care program: new hospitals were built and mental health facilities were upgraded. New power-producing facilities, such as the Fontana Dam at the edge of the Great Smoky Mountains (1945) and Kerr Dam near Henderson (1953), provided electricity for industry. Because of these improvements, more businesses began coming into North Carolina—nearly 150 new industries in 1956 alone. And higher education in the state was keeping in step. In 1958 three of the state's top schools—

Duke University in Durham, the University of North Carolina at Chapel Hill, and North Carolina State University at Raleigh—pooled their resources to form the North Carolina Research Triangle, which provided research and advice to industry.

Beginning in 1954 and lasting through the 1970s, public schools were desegregated following U.S. Supreme Court and congressional decisions. In 1971 a lower court order for busing pupils to maintain racial desegregation was upheld by the U.S. Supreme Court. It was not until 1981 that North Carolina and the U.S. Department of Education agreed on a plan for complete desegregation of the North Carolina State University system by 1986.

Today, new industries continue to come into the Tar Heel State (as it was nicknamed during the Civil War, when North Carolina troops threatened to put tar on the heels of other Southern soldiers who left them to fight alone—so that they would "stick better in the next fight"). Forest products are an important part of the economy. Agriculture remains strong, with emphasis on tobacco, soybeans, poultry and eggs, peanuts, cotton, and potatoes. Manufacturing has diversified into chemicals, plastics, and electronics in addition to furniture, textiles, tobacco products and food processing. The beautiful Blue Ridge Mountains and other scenic areas attract vacationers to North Carolina for swimming, boating, camping, hunting, and fishing. Other recreational facilities include excellent golf courses, historic towns, four national forests, and a dozen state parks.

The People

Slightly more than 40 percent of the residents of North Carolina live in or near cities and towns, and more than one half of all Tar Heels live in metropolitan areas. Approximately 98 percent of North Carolinians were born in the United States. The largest religious group in the state is the Baptist denomination. Methodists rank second, with Presbyterians third.

Famous People

Many famous people were born in the state of North Carolina. Here are a few:

Luke Appling b. 1907, High Point. Hall of Fame baseball player

Thomas Hart Benton 1782-1858, Hillsboro. Senator who fought the extension of slavery into new territories

Braxton Bragg 1817-1876, Warren County. Confederate general

David Brinkley b. 1920, Wilmington. Television news anchorman

Robert Byrd b. 1917, North Wilkesboro. Senate majority leader

Joseph Cannon 1836-1926, Guilford. Speaker of the House of Representatives, 1903-1911

Thomas Lanier Clingman 1812-1902, Huntersville. Soldier and politician

John Coltrane 1926-1967, Hamlet. Jazz saxophonist

Howard Cosell b. 1920,

Born in North Carolina, Missouri senator Thomas Hart Benton was a leader in the anti-slavery movement before the Civil War.

Winston-Salem. Television sportscaster

Charlie Daniels b. 1936, Wilmington. Country singer

Josephus Daniels 1862-1948, Washington. Journalist, Secretary of the Navy, and Ambassador to Mexico

Virginia Dare 1587-?, Roanoke Island. The first child born in America of English parents

Walter Davis b. 1954, Pineville. Basketball player

Elizabeth Hanford Dole b. 1936, Salisbury. Secretary of Transportation in Reagan and Bush cabinets

Benjamin N. Duke 1855-1929, Durham. Tobacco executive and benefactor of Duke University

James B. Duke 1856-1925, Durham. Tobacco

Howard Cosell, best known as a sportscaster, received his law degree from New York University, where he was editor of the Law Review.

Elizabeth Dole, now the president of the American Red Cross, graduated from Duke University, where she was president of the student body.

executive and benefactor of Duke University

Samuel Ervin 1896-1985, Morgantown. Senator who led the Watergate investigation

Homer L. Ferguson 1873-1952, Waynesville. Shipbuilder who made many World War II naval vessels

Roberta Flack b. 1939, Black Mountain. Pop singer

Roman Gabriel b. 1940, Wilmington. Football player.

Ava Gardner 1922-1990, Smithfield. Film actress: *On the Beach, Showboat*

Richard J. Gatling 1818-1903, Hertford County. Inventor of the machine gun

Billy Graham b. 1918, Charlotte. Southern Baptist evangelist

Andy Griffith b. 1926, Mount Airy. Television actor: *The Andy Griffith Show, Matlock*

George Grizzard b. 1928, Roanoke Rapids. Stage and film actor: *Advise and Consent, Wrong is Right*

O. Henry (William Sidney Porter) 1862-1910, Greensboro. Short story writer: "The Gift of the Magi," "The Ransom of Red Chief"

James "Catfish" Hunter b. 1946, Hertford. Hall of Fame baseball pitcher

Andrew Johnson 1808-1875, Raleigh. Seventeenth President of the United States

Christian "Sonny" Jurgenson b. 1934, Wilmington. Hall of Fame football player

Charley "Choo Choo" Justice b. 1924, Asheville. Football player

Charles Kuralt b. 1934, Bishop. Broadcast journalist

O. Henry wrote his first short stories while in prison for embezzlement.

Sugar Ray Leonard b. 1956,
Wilmington. Welterweight
boxing champion

Dolley Madison 1768-1849,
Guilford County. Wife of
President James Madison

Bob McAdoo b. 1951,
Greensboro. Basketball
player

Ronnie Milsap b. 1943,
Robinsville. Country-and-
western singer

*Sonny Jurgenson still holds the
Washington Redskins record for
touchdown passes in a single season;
he threw 31 scoring passes during
the 1967 season.*

*Sugar Ray Leonard came into
prominence as an Olympic boxing
gold medalist in 1976.*

Thelonious Monk 1920-1982,
Rocky Mount. Jazz pianist

Edward R. Murrow 1908-
1965, Greensboro. War
correspondent and
broadcast journalist

Floyd Patterson 1935-1989,
Waco. Heavyweight
boxing champion

Gaylord Perry b. 1938,
Williamston. Baseball
pitcher

Richard Petty b. 1937,

Randleman.
Championship auto racer

James K. Polk 1795-1849,
Mecklenburg County.
Eleventh President of the
United States

Hiram R. Revels 1822-1901,
Fayetteville. The first black
elected to the U.S. Senate

Max Roach b. 1924, Elizabeth
City. Jazz percussionist

Robert Ruark 1915-1965,
Wilmington. Novelist:

*Dolley Madison saved many state
documents when Washington D.C.
was burned by the British in 1814.*

Something of Value, The Honey Badger

Soupy Sales b. 1926, Franklinton. Television comedian

Don Schollander b. 1946, Charlotte. Olympic gold-medal winning swimmer

Nina Simone b. 1933, Tyron. Jazz singer and pianist

Elbridge A. Stuart 1856-1944, Guilford County. Founder of the Carnation Company, maker of evaporated milk and other groceries

Billy Taylor b. 1921, Greenville. Jazz pianist and orchestra leader

David Thompson b. 1954, Shelby. Basketball player

Tom Wicker b. 1926, Hamlet. *New York Times* columnist

Hoyt Wilhelm b. 1923, Huntersville. Hall of Fame baseball player

Thomas Wolfe 1900-1938, Asheville. Novelist: *Look Homeward, Angel; You Can't Go Home Again*

James K. Polk's rise to power was linked to his belief in expansionism; he favored the annexation of Texas and the acquisition of the Oregon territory.

Colleges and Universities

There are many colleges and universities in North Carolina. Here are the most prominent, with their locations, dates of founding, and enrollments.

Appalachian State University, Boone, 1903, 650

Native sons James K. Polk and Andrew Johnson, along with Andrew Jackson born in neighboring South Carolina, are honored by the Three Presidents Statue in Raleigh.

Thomas Wolfe grew up in this boarding house in Asheville; his first novel, Look Homeward, Angel, *drew upon some of his childhood experiences.*

Barton College, Wilson, 1902, 1,720

Belmont Abbey College, Belmont, 1878, 1,016

Campbell University, Buies Creek, 1887, 5,806

Catawba College, Salisbury, 1851, 962

Davidson College, Davidson, 1837, 1,550

Duke University, Durham, 1838, 11,426

East Carolina University, Greenville, 1907, 17,757

Elizabeth City State University, Elizabeth City, 1891, 2,100

Elon College, Elon, 1889, 3,227

Greensboro College, Greensboro, 1838, 1,000

Guilford College, Greensboro, 1834, 1,202

High Point College, High Point, 1924, 2,326

James C. Smith University, Charlotte, 1867, 1,165

Lenoir Rhyne College, Hickory, 1891, 1,522

Livingstone College, Salisbury, 1879, 642

Meredith College, Raleigh, 1891, 2,049

North Carolina Agricultural and Technical State University, Greensboro, 1891, 7,580

North Carolina Central University, Durham, 1910, 5,385

North Carolina State University, Raleigh, 1887, 27,156

North Carolina Wesleyan College, Rocky Mount, 1956, 650

Pembroke State University, Pembroke, 1887, 3,041

Pfeiffer College, Misenheimer, 1887, 916

The chapel at Duke University in Durham. Founded in 1838, the Women's College was added in 1925.

Queens College, Charlotte, 1857, 1,602

St. Andrews Presbyterian College, Laurinberg, 1857, 716

St. Augustine's College, Raleigh, 1867, 1,918

Salem College, Winston-Salem, 1772, 842

University of North Carolina— at Asheville, 1927, 3,277; at Chapel Hill, 1789, 23,944; at Charlotte, 1946, 15,363; at Greensboro, 1891, 12,117; at Wilmington, 1947, 7,898

Wake Forest University, Winston-Salem, 1834, 5,624

Western Carolina University, Cullowhee, 1889, 6,576

Winston-Salem State University, Winston-Salem, 1892, 2,655

Where To Get More Information
The Travel and
Tourism Division
430 North Salisbury Street
Raleigh, NC 27603
or call 1-800-VISITNC

South Carolina

The state seal of South Carolina, adopted in 1776, is circular. On the left side of the circle is an oval containing a drawing of a palmetto tree (symbolizing the fort on Sullivan's Island built of palmetto logs) rising from a torn-up oak tree trunk (symbolizing the British fleet that was beaten by the men in the fort on June 28, 1776). Toward the bottom of the palmetto is a plaque with the words *Quis Separabit*, or "Who Shall Separate?" Under the oak is enscribed *Meliorem Lapsa Locavit*, or "Having Fallen It has Set Up Better." Under this is the date 1776, the date of the first independent South Carolina constitution. Around the oval is written South Carolina and the motto *Animis Opibusque Parati*, or "Prepared in mind and resources."

On the right side of the circle is an oval containing a drawing of Hope, carrying a laurel branch across a sword-covered beach with the rising sun behind her, symbolizing the wish to remain forever independent. Under the drawing is the word *Spes*, Latin for "Hope," and above the oval is written the other state motto, *Dum Spiro Spero*, "While I breathe, I hope."

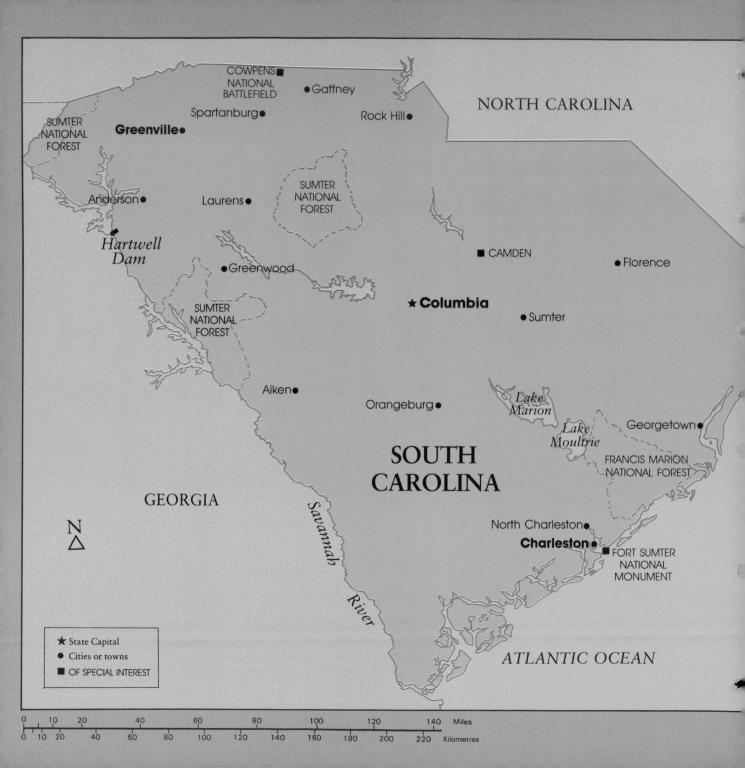

SOUTH CAROLINA
At a Glance

Capital: Columbia

State Flag

State Bird:
Carolina Wren

State Flower:
Carolina Jessamine

Size: 31,113 square miles (40th largest)
Population: 3,603,227 (25th largest)

Major Crops: Tobacco, soybeans, corn, cotton, hay

State Flag

The first state flag of South Carolina was designed in 1775 by Colonel William Moultrie. It was blue, as were the uniforms of the South Carolina troops in the Revolutionary War. At the upper right was a crescent of silver. Later, after the Battle of Sullivan's Island and the palmetto fort, a palmetto tree was added in the center. The present flag is the same, except that the crescent is now in the upper left corner.

Distant mountains provide a backdrop for South Carolina fall foliage.

State Mottoes

Animis Opibusque Parati, Dum Spiro Spero

These two mottoes were selected in 1776, after South Carolina declared itself to be an independent colony. *Animis Opibusque Parati* is Latin for "Prepared in Mind and Resources," and *Dum Spiro Spero* is Latin for "While I Breathe, I Hope." Together, they symbolize the determination, strength, and hope of the citizens of South Carolina.

State Name and Nicknames

Both South and North Carolina were once a single territory called Carolina, named to honor King Charles I of England. The Latin version of Charles is *Carolus*. Carolinus is an adjective form of the name, and Carolina is the feminine form of the adjective.

South Carolina has several nicknames. It is a leader in the production of rice, so it is often called the *Rice State* and the *Swamp State*. Because the state has roughly the shape of a wedge, it has been called the *Keystone of the South Atlantic Seaboard*. Since many native South Carolina plants contain iodine, it has also been called the *Iodine State*. Finally, since the state tree is the palmetto, it is most commonly called the *Palmetto State*.

State Capital

From 1670 to 1790, Charleston was the capital of South Carolina. Columbia was made the capital in 1790.

State Flower

The yellow jessamine (family *Loganiaceae*) was named the state flower of South Carolina by the general assembly in 1924. It is fragrant and resilient, and grows all over the state.

State Tree

The state tree is the palmetto, *Inodes palmetto*, which was adopted officially in 1939. It has a long association with the state and appears on the state flag and state seal.

State Bird

The Carolina wren (family Troglodytidae) had long been the unofficial state bird until 1939, when the legislature unexpectedly named the mockingbird, *Mimus polyglottis*, the official state bird. The act was repealed, and the Carolina wren was finally adopted in 1948.

State Animal

The white-tailed deer, *Odocoileus virginianus*, was selected as the state animal in 1972.

State Beverage

Milk was adopted as the state beverage in 1984.

State Dance

In 1984, the shag was named the state dance.

State Dog

The Boykin Spaniel, originally bred in South Carolina for hunting, was designated state dog in 1985.

State Fish

The striped bass, *Roccus*

Cotton, grown primarily in the coastal region, is one of the principle crops of South Carolina.

The palmetto is sometimes known as the cabbage palm.

saxatilis, also called the rockfish, was selected as the state fish in 1972.

State Fruit
The peach (family *Rosaceae)* has been the state fruit since 1984.

State Gemstone
In 1969 the amethyst, a form of quartz, was adopted as the state gemstone.

State Shell
The lettered olive, *Oliva sayana*, was named state shell in 1984.

State Stone
Blue granite was adopted as the state stone in 1969.

State Pledge of Allegiance
In 1966, the general assembly named a pledge of allegiance to the state flag: "I salute the flag of South Carolina and pledge to the Palmetto State love, loyalty and faith."

Blue granite, the state stone of South Carolina.

State Song

South Carolina has two state songs. In 1911, "Carolina," with words by Henry Timrod and music by Anne Custis Burgess, was adopted. In 1984, the state added "South Carolina on My Mind," written and recorded by Hank Martin and Buzz Arledge.

State Wild Game Bird

The wild turkey, *Meleagris gallopavo*, was chosen as state wild game bird in 1976.

Population

The population of South Carolina in 1992 was 3,603,227, making it the 25th most populous state. There are 119.7 persons per square mile. About 98 percent of South Carolinians were born in the United States, and some 80 percent of them were born in South Carolina. The largest groups born in other countries are British and German.

Industries

The principal industries of the state of South Carolina are tourism, agriculture, textiles, chemicals and allied products, machinery, fabricated metal products, and apparel.

Agriculture

The chief crops of the state are tobacco, soybeans, corn, cotton, peaches, and hay. South Carolina is also a livestock state. There are estimated to be some 575,000 cattle; 410,000 hogs and pigs; and 7.13 million chickens on its farms. Pine and oak are harvested for timber, and cement, crushed stone, clay, sand, and gravel are important mineral resources. In 1992 commercial fishing earned $25.6 million. With 26.2 percent of South Carolinians employed in manufacturing, the state is second in the country in the percent of people employed in this sector. In 1991 tourism earned $6.4 billion in South Carolina.

Government

The governor of South Carolina is elected to a four-year term, as are the lieutenant governor, adjutant general, attorney general, commissioner of agriculture, comptroller general, secretary of state, state treasurer, and superintendent of education. The general assembly consists of a 46-member senate and a 124-member house of representatives. Each of the state's 46 counties sends a senator for a four-year term to Columbia, and each county elects from one to 11 representatives for a two-year term. The most recent state constitution was adopted in 1895. In addition to its two U.S. senators, South Carolina has six representatives in the U.S. House of Representatives. The state has nine votes in the electoral college.

Sports

Sporting events on the collegiate and secondary school levels may be seen all over the state. On the collegiate level, Clemson University won the Orange Bowl games of 1951 and 1982. Fishing on lakes and rivers, as well as surf casting and deep-water fishing, are available year-round. Hunting, camping, hiking, and white-water rafting are also popular.

Major Cities

Charleston (population 80,467). Founded in 1670, it boasts a fine harbor, described by natives as "where the Ashley and Cooper rivers unite to form the Atlantic Ocean." In its early days, the city served as an example of European luxury and culture in the New World. The oldest city in the state, it was the site of the first theater to present drama exclusively, the first

Tobacco is another of South Carolina's major crops.

The Charleston Battery district offers some fine examples of a typically Charlestonian design element, the multi-storied piazza, or porch.

museum in the colony, the first municipal college in the country, and the first fire insurance company in North America.

Places to visit in Charleston: White Point Gardens, the Edmondston-Alston House (1828), the Old Exchange and Provost Dungeon (1771), the Heyward-Washington House (1772), Old Slave Mart Museum and Gallery, the Huguenot Church (1845), St. Philip's Church (1838),

Gateway Walk, the Powder Magazine (1713), the Gibbes Museum of Art, the Thomas Elfe Workshop (1760), the City Hall Art Gallery (1801), St. Michael's Church (1751), the Nathaniel Russell House (1808), the Calhoun Mansion, the Chamber of Commerce (1862), St. Mary's Church (1839), Kahal Kadosh Beth Elohim (1840), the Unitarian Church (1772), St. John's Lutheran Church (1817), the Circular Congregational Church (1891), the Charleston Museum (1773), the Joseph

Manigault House (1803), the Aiken-Rhett Mansion (1817), the Charles Towne Landing, Hampton Park, the aircraft carrier Yorktown — Patriots Point, Naval and Maritime Museum, Fort Sumter, the Boone Hall Plantation (1681), Drayton Hall (1738), the Magnolia Plantation and Gardens, the Middleton Place Gardens—House and Stableyards, Cypress Gardens, Palmetto Islands County Park, and Francis Beidler Forest.

Columbia (population 103,477). Founded in 1786, the city is not only the state capital, but also the state's wholesale and retail center. It was rebuilt after 1865, when General Sherman's troops had reduced it to ashes.

Places to visit in Columbia: the State House, Trinity Cathedral (1847) and Churchyard, the Town Theatre (1919), the Columbia Museum of Art, the Gibbes Planetarium, the First Presbyterian Church (1853), the First Baptist Church (1856), the Governor's Mansion (1855), the Marshal-De Bruhl House (1820), the

Mann-Simons Cottage (1850), the Woodrow Wilson Boyhood Home (1872), the Confederate Relic Room and Museum, the Hampton-Preston Mansion (1818), the Robert Mills Historic House (1823), the McKissick Museum, Riverbanks Zoological Park, Sherman's Battery, Fort Jackson, the Lexington County Museum Complex, Sesquicentennial State Park, and Congaree Swamp National Monument.

Places to Visit

The National Park Service maintains six areas in the state of South Carolina: Kings Mountain National Military Park, Cowpens National Battlefield, Fort Sumter National Monument, Ninety-Six National Historic Site, Francis Marion National Forest, and Sumter National Forest. In addition, there are 37 state recreation areas.

Aiken: Hopeland Gardens. This public garden includes flowers, sculptures, reflecting pools, and terraces.

Anderson: Pendleton Historic District. Forty-five historic homes and buildings can be

The Riverbanks Zoo in Columbia is home to more than 2,000 animals, and draws more than one million visitors a year.

toured in this city settled in 1790.

Beaufort: John Mark Verdier House Museum. Once known as the Lafayette Building, it was built in the late 1790s.

Camden: Historic Camden. Nineteenth-century log cabins and a restored eighteenth-century town house are found in the archeological site of the colonial town.

Cheraw: Historic District. Nearly 50 homes and public buildings, dating to before the Civil War, are found here.

Clinton: Rose Hill. Dating from 1828, this is a restored cotton plantation.

Florence: Air and Missile Museum. Aircraft and missiles of all kinds are displayed here.

Georgetown: Hopsewee Plantation. Dating from 1740, this preserved rice plantation and house was the birthplace of Thomas Lynch, Jr., a signer of the Declaration of Independence.

Greenwood: Gardens of Park Seed Company. Some 1,600 varieties of flowers and vegetables are on display.

Hartsville: Kalmia Gardens of Coker College. Visitors may tour a backwater swamp, mountain laurel thickets, pine-oak-holly uplands, and a beech bluff.

Orangeburg: Edisto Memorial Gardens. This is a 101-acre site with more than 3200 azaleas, camellias, rose bushes, and flowering trees.

Rock Hill: Museum of York County. A large collection of mounted African hoofed mammals is displayed, as well as local artifacts.

Sumter: Church of the Holy Cross. Constructed of rammed earth in 1850, the church has beautiful stained-glass windows.

Walterboro: Colleton County Courthouse. The first public meeting in the state in support of states' rights over federal law was held here in 1828.

Events

There are many events and organizations that schedule activities of various kinds in the state of South Carolina. Here are some of them.

Sports: Triple Crown horse racing (Aiken); Polo Games (Aiken); horse racing at the Springdale Race Course (Camden); TransSouth 500 stock car race (Darlington); Southern 500 stock car classic (Darlington); Freedom Weekend Aloft (Greenville); Family Circle Magazine Cup Tennis

Tournament (Hilton Head Island); MCI Heritage Classic (Hilton Head Island); Hilton Head Island Celebrity Golf Tournament (Hilton Head Island); Hyatt 10-Kilometer Run (Hilton Head Island); Fishing Rodeo (Myrtle Beach); Arthur Smith King Mackerel Tournament (Myrtle Beach);

Metropolitan Columbia, the state's capital and largest city, possesses a wide assortment of museums and parks.

Coon Hunt (Orangeburg).

Arts and Crafts: Southeastern Wildlife Exposition (Charleston); Spring Festival (Cheraw); Arts Alive (Florence); South Carolina Peach Festival (Gaffney); Festival of Flowers (Greenwood); South Carolina Festival of Roses (Orangeburg); Come-See-Me (Rock Hill); Sumter Iris Festival (Sumter); Fall Fiesta of the Arts (Sumter).

Music: Charleston Symphony (Charleston); Spoleto Festival, USA (Charleston).

Entertainment: Anderson Fair (Anderson); Beaufort Water Festival (Beaufort); Palmetto Balloon Classic (Camden); South Carolina State Fair (Columbia); Sweet Potato Festival (Darlington); Hartscapades Festival (Hartsville); Springfest (Hilton Head Island); Sun Fun Festival (Myrtle Beach); Orangeburg County Fair (Orangeburg); Piedmont Interstate Fair (Spartanburg); Rice Festival (Walterboro).

Tours: St. Thaddeus Tour of Homes (Aiken); Tour of Homes and Gardens (Beaufort); Festival of Houses (Charleston); Fall House and Garden Candlelight Tours (Charleston); St. Luke's Tour of Homes (Hilton Head Island).

Theater: Dock Street Theatre (Charleston); Town Theatre (Columbia).

Myrtle Beach is a favorite year-round vacation spot.

Hilton Head, a popular year-round resort, is host to several major sports tournaments.

Dense foliage, rocky hills, and waterfalls are typical of the high ground that covers most of northwestern South Carolina.

The Atlantic Coastal Plain, which covers the southeastern two-thirds of the state, contains a great many of South Carolina's wide bays and rivers.

The Land and the Climate

Although South Carolina is the smallest of the southern states, it has three main land regions: the Atlantic Coastal Plain, the Piedmont, and the Blue Ridge. Natives of the state call the Atlantic Coastal Plain the Low Country and the Piedmont and Blue Ridge the Up Country.

The Atlantic Coastal Plain is part of the long shelf-like formation that stretches from New York to Florida: it covers the southeastern two-thirds of the state. The plain rises gradually from southeast to northwest; near the Atlantic coast it is flat, but broken by wide bays and rivers. Huge swamps cover most of the coastal area and extend inland along the rivers. The Atlantic Coastal Plain also takes in the Pine Barrens, a belt of evergreen forests. Running through Aiken, Camden, Cheraw, and Columbia is a series of sand hills, which mark the western edge of the plain. There is evidence that these sand hills were once part of an ancient beach, which means that the plain probably lay beneath the ocean thousands of years ago. This low country produces one of the state's most important crops—tobacco. Kaolin and other clays are found here, and limestone quarries produce stone for building.

A canoeist riding the rapids of the Chattooga River, located in the northwestern tip of the state. Rivers such as the Chattooga, Saluda, and Enoree provide South Carolina with much of its hydroelectric power.

The Piedmont covers most of northwestern South Carolina, comprising part of a hilly region adjoining mountain ranges from New York to Alabama. It is high ground, and rivers flow swiftly from the Up Country to the Atlantic Coastal Plain. The southeast part of the Piedmont is a rolling upland, whose altitudes range from 400 to 1,000 feet above sea level. At the western edge of the Piedmont, heights can reach 1,500 feet. The fast-flowing rivers of the Piedmont area are a prime source of hydroelectric power, making this the most important manufacturing area of the state, whose abundant water supply is its major natural resource.

The Blue Ridge is in the northwest corner of South Carolina, and it, too, is part of a larger land formation that runs from southern Pennsylvania to northern Georgia. The region is named for the Blue Ridge Mountains—part of the Appalachian system—which extend down from North Carolina. However, the South Carolina Blue Ridge Mountains are not as high as those in the neighboring state; all of them are forested to the top, indicating their lesser altitude. Sassafras Mountain is the highest in the state, at 3,560 feet above sea level.

When the coastline of South Carolina is measured in a straight line, it totals 187 miles. But the coast is so riddled with bays, harbors, and inlets that if the actual length of land bordering salt water were added together, it would total 2,876 miles. The important bays from north to south are Little River Inlet, Winyah Bay, Bull Bay, Charleston Harbor, St. Helena Sound, and Port Royal Sound.

Among the many islands off the coast of the South Carolina mainland, from north to south, are Pawley's and Bull Islands; Isle of Palms; and Sullivan, Edisto, Hunting, Fripps, and Hilton Head Islands. Near Beaufort is Parris Island, a major training center for the United States Marines.

Riverboats like the *Carolina* were once the prime mode of transportation in the region. They are now used mainly for recreational purposes.

Hilton Head, on the southernmost coast of South Carolina, is one of the most popular resorts in the region.

Although the Blue Ridge Mountains run through both North and South Carolina, they differ in the two states. In South Carolina, the mountains are forested to the top, indicating their lower altitude.

The Pee Dee River is the largest of those rivers that flow from northwest to southeast across the state. Other major waterways are the Santee, Savannah, Broad, and Saluda Rivers. Many beautiful waterfalls have formed on the rivers of the steep Blue Ridge region. South Carolina has no large natural lakes, but dams have created many large man-made lakes in their reservoirs. The largest is Lake Marion; others include Catawba, Greenwood, Moultrie, Murray, and Wateree Lakes.

Because of its proximity to the Atlantic Ocean, the eastern half of South Carolina is warm and humid; the western section is drier. Temperatures range between 70 and 92 degrees Fahrenheit in summer and drop to 35 to 58 degrees F. in winter. Rainfall averages 46 inches yearly, most of which falls in the mountains. The state has little snowfall—rarely more than a few inches, except in the mountains. Even they receive less than a foot of snow per year.

The History

Before the first Spaniards arrived in what is now South Carolina, more than 30 Indian tribes were living there, most of them in semi-permanent log shelters near the land that they farmed. The most important tribes were the Catawba, the Cherokee, and the Yamasee (or Yemasee). The Catawba belonged to the Siouan Indian language family, the Cherokee to the Iroquoian, and the Yamasee to the Muskhogean language family.

Possibly the first white men to visit the area were the Spaniards Francisco Gordillo and his men. Gordillo was the leader of an expedition that explored the coast of South Carolina in 1521; it had come from Spanish-held Santo Domingo, a Caribbean city on Hispaniola Island in what is now the Dominican Republic. Then came Lucas Vásquez de Ayllón, a judge from Santo Domingo, who set up a colony in what is now the Winyah Bay area near Georgetown. Five hundred men, women, and children tried to survive there, but because of disease and bad weather, they returned to Santo Domingo. The French tried to settle at Port Royal and farther south (1562–5), but these colonies failed too, mostly because of the lack of food.

Then it was the turn of the English. John Cabot had sailed for the English in 1497, and the British felt that his voyage of exploration had given them a claim to all of North America. Accordingly, in 1629, King Charles I of England granted some North American land to Sir Robert Heath, including what would become South and North Carolina. (The grant was supposed to extend westward to the edge of the continent.) The eastern portion was named the Province of Carolana (Land of Charles), but the spelling was changed to Carolina in 1663. However, Heath seemed reluctant to establish colonies in his territories.

Guides in period costume depict colonial life at Charles Town Landing, site of the first permanent English settlement in South Carolina. Visitors can board a 17th-century trading ship, or stroll through an authentic village where many popular herbs and plants of the time are grown.

In 1663 Charles's son, Charles II, gave Carolina to eight English noblemen who were called the lords proprietors. These men sent settlers to the New World, and in 1670 the immigrants established the first permanent white settlement in South Carolina at Albemarle Point, near what is now Charleston. The settlers moved to Oyster Point, which they named Charles Town, in 1680. (The spelling was changed to Charleston after the Revolutionary War.)

South Carolinians, along the coast, were particularly vulnerable to attack during Queen Anne's War (1702–13), but they successfully defended themselves against French and Spanish invaders in a battle at

Charles Town. They also fought with the local Yamasee Indians and repelled attacks by pirates between 1715 and 1718. The proprietors gave them little in the way of either arms or troops, because they feared a move toward self-government. In 1719 the resentful colonists requested that certain laws be passed for their benefit. When the proprietors rejected the request, the settlers rebelled.

King George I of England bought back Carolina from the proprietors in 1721, because the region was a British bulwark against French and Spanish settlements to the south. Thus Carolina became a royal colony with a modest amount of self-government. The area was divided into two provinces—South and North Carolina—in 1730. Two years later the southern part of South Carolina became the colony of Georgia.

In the mid-1700s, there was a wave of immigration to the Up Country of South Carolina—not only from eastern South Carolina, but from Pennsylvania and Virginia. The population of the colony was nearly 170,000 by 1775. This included about 70,000 whites and 100,000 blacks, most of whom were slaves, captured in Africa and shipped in to work on rice and cotton plantations.

Oppressive laws passed by the English parliament in the 1760s irritated the people of South Carolina as well as residents of the other 12 colonies. Most of these statutes were heavy tax levies designed to help pay for the expensive colonial wars, or laws that restricted trade in the Americas. Those settlers loyal to the British Crown became known as Tories, and those opposed were called Whigs. The Whigs predominated in South Carolina.

After the Revolutionary War began in Massachusetts (1775), the colonists in South Carolina were still divided in their loyalties, but many important battles were fought in the colony. In June, 1776, the British attempted to capture Charleston, a valuable port, from both land and sea. They were defeated by the Whigs in the Battle of Fort Moultrie. In 1779 the British attacked Charleston again, without success. On the third attempt (1780) the English troops finally captured

A few cannons still stand at Fort Moultrie, where, soon after the start of the Revolutionary War, American patriots defeated British troops who were attempting to capture the valuable port of Charleston.

A portrait of Francis Marion, an American general in the Revolutionary War. After Charleston was lost to the British, Marion accepted a commission as brigadier general of the South Carolina militia. He gathered a band of rugged cavalrymen and, with surprise attacks and lightning-swift retreats into protecting woods and swamps, rattled the enemy by freeing compatriots and breaking British communication lines. Marion's skill at negotiating South Carolina's difficult terrain earned him the nickname "Swamp Fox."

the city, and that August they defeated American troops under the command of General Horatio Gates at Camden. As a result, the British and the Tories controlled most of the colony.

The tide of war turned in the colonists' favor at the Battles of Kings Mountain (October 7, 1780) and Cowpens (January 17, 1781). Then General Nathanael Greene drove the British troops into Virginia with his colonial army. South Carolina militiamen led by officers who knew the state's difficult terrain—Francis Marion (called the Swamp Fox), Thomas Sumter (nicknamed the Gamecock), and Andrew Pickens—defeated smaller British units and liberated Charleston in 1782. During the War for Independence, some 137 battles and skirmishes were fought in South Carolina. On July 9, 1778, South Carolina approved the Articles of Confederation, which united the former 13 colonies under a federal government. On May 23, 1788, the state became the eighth to ratify the Constitution of the United States.

South Carolina was a strong supporter of states' rights, and bitterly opposed federal tariffs because its economy depended so heavily on trade with European countries. When an economic depression hit in the 1820s and the Federal Government set up trade restrictions, South Carolina adopted an ordinance of nullification, refusing to follow the tariff laws until after 1833.

In the 1840s the anti-slavery movement in the North became increasingly strong: by 1850 the dispute over whether or not slavery was to be extended westward was beginning to come to a head. South Carolina threatened to secede, or withdraw, from the Union, but could get little support from the other southern states. Then, on November 6, 1860, Abraham Lincoln, a Northern Republican, was elected President of the United States, and South Carolina feared that he would try to abolish slavery. As a result, South Carolina was the first state to secede from the Union, on December 20, 1860. By the following Spring, 10 other southern states had joined it to form the Confederate States of America. The Civil War began in South Carolina on April 12, 1861, when Confederate troops fired on the Union troops who were stationed in Fort Sumter in Charleston Harbor.

A portrait of Thomas Sumter, a patriot leader of the American Revolution. Originally a justice of the peace near Eutaw Springs, Sumter participated in the early Carolina campaigns of the Revolution. After the fall of Charleston, he was elected general of a guerilla force that harassed the British occupation forces. His nickname, "the Gamecock," was given to him by his men in recognition of his fighting spirit.

The remains of Fort Sumter in Charleston Harbor, where the first shots of the Civil War were fired by Confederate forces in 1861.

Many battles were fought in South Carolina during the Civil War, mostly along the coast. The Union Navy blockaded Charleston Harbor and killed the state's economy by cutting off maritime trade. Union troops under General William Tecumseh Sherman destroyed many plantations in the state and burned Columbia, the capital, in 1865. By the end of the war, South Carolina had sent about 63,000 men into battle, at least 25 percent of whom were killed.

After the Civil War, Union troops occupied the South during the bitter period known as Reconstruction. It was not until 1868 that South Carolina adopted a new constitution, giving blacks the right to vote, and was readmitted to the Union. Even then, federal troops remained in the state until 1877, and Republicans with Northern sympathies dominated its government.

In the late 1800s, South Carolina began to recover from the destructive effects of the Civil War and to embark upon a period of industrial growth. Farm income had declined because of competition from new farms farther west, but around 1880, South Carolina textile-mill owners began expanding their factories, utilizing an abundant supply of water power for thier energy needs. Thousands of men left their farms to work in the textile mills, and because they made up a work force that would settle for low wages, many Northern textile companies moved into the state. These mills produced huge amounts of cloth goods for the armed forces of the United States after it entered World War I in 1917. By 1920, the year after the war ended, over 54,000 people were employed by South Carolina textile mills.

Because of a severe boll weevil epidemic in the 1920s, many South Carolina farmers switched from cotton—their main crop since colonial days—to fruits, tobacco, wheat, and other farm products. The Great Depression of the 1930s caused widespread unemployment in manufacturing and financial hardship for farming families as well. Franklin D. Roosevelt's New Deal, whereby the Federal Government took a major role in economic recovery, helped both the state and the nation.

This spiral staircase in the Nathaniel Russell House is typical of the grand architecture of early 19th-century Charleston. The house was built in 1808 by Nathaniel Russell, who had amassed a fortune in shipping from the South's busiest and most cosmopolitan port. Charleston became a center of innovative architecture during the late 1700s and early 1800s.

St. Philip's Episcopal Church in Charleston, the first church established in the colony. In its churchyard are buried John C. Calhoun, former vice-president, Edward Rutledge, a signer of the Declaration of Independence, and DuBose Heyward, author of the novel *Porgy*.

When the United States entered World War II in 1941, South Carolina textiles and farm products were in demand again. In 1942 the South Carolina Public Service Authority completed the Santee-Cooper Navigation Canal and Power Dam between the Santee and Cooper Rivers. The project created Lake Marion and Lake Moultrie as well as a new source of hydroelectric power that gave a boost to industry in the state.

During the twentieth century, the economy of South Carolina has changed greatly. In the early 1900s, the state's prosperity depended mainly on one cash crop, cotton, and one industry, textiles. Cotton is still important today, but so are peaches, soybeans, and tobacco. And while textiles remain a major source of revenue, chemicals, electrical machinery, and paper products have diversified the manufacturing scene. With its aristocratic and romantic past, South Carolina has the additional attraction of historic sites and scenic beauties that extend to every corner of the state: Charleston Harbor, antebellum plantations and gardens, the Blue Ridge mountains. The economic revolution of the twentieth century has not spoiled the romance of the Old South that is found everywhere in the Palmetto State.

One of the first plays performed in America by professional actors was staged at the Dock Street Theater in Charleston. When it opened in 1736, it was the only building in the country devoted entirely to drama. It was also host to America's first production of a play by Shakespeare.

The People

Today, approximately 60 percent of the people in South Carolina live in or near the cities and towns. About 98 percent of South Carolinians were born in the United States. Most of those who are foreign-born came from Great Britain and Germany. South Carolina has one of the highest percentages of church members in proportion to population. Most residents are Protestant, and Baptists outnumber all other religious groups. Other denominations include the Episcopal, Lutheran, Methodist, Presbyterian, and Roman Catholic.

Famous People

Many famous people were born in the state of South Carolina. Here are a few:

Washington Allston 1779-1843, near Georgetown. Painter and poet

Bernard Baruch 1870-1965, Camden. Financial advisor to every President from Wilson to Kennedy

Mary McLeod Bethune 1875-1955, Mayesville. One of the founders of Bethune-Cookman College

James F. Byrnes 1879-1972, Charleston. Senator and justice of the U.S. Supreme Court

John C. Calhoun 1782-1850, Abbeville District. Representative, senator, and vice-president under John Quincy Adams

Althea Gibson b. 1927, Silver. Tennis champion

Dizzy Gillespie 1917-93, Cheraw. Jazz trumpeter

Angelina Emily Grimké 1805-1879, Charleston. Abolitionist

Sarah Moore Grimké 1792-1873, Charleston. Abolitionist

Wade Hampton 1818-1902, Charleston. Confederate cavalry commander

Bernard Baruch began his financial career in a Wall Street brokerage house. His first government appointment was to President Woodrow Wilson's Council of National Defense in 1916.

DuBose Heyward 1885-1940, Charleston. Poet and novelist: *Porgy, Peter Ashley*

Lauren Hutton b. 1944, Charleston. Model and film actress

Andrew Jackson 1767-1845, Waxhaw. Seventh President of the United States

Jesse Jackson b. 1941, Greenville. Civil rights leader and clergyman

Dizzy Gillespie was one of the leaders of the bop movement of the 1940s.

Andrew Jackson was born on a frontier settlement, and received little formal schooling until he began to study law at the age of seventeen.

"Shoeless" Joe Jackson 1848-1951, Pickens County. Baseball player

Eartha Kitt b. 1928, North. Singer and stage actress

Henry Laurens 1724-92, Charleston. Political leader

James Longstreet 1821-1904, Edgefield district. Confederate general

Francis Marion 1731-1795, Winyah. Revolutionary War general

Samuel Maverick 1803-1870, Pendleton. Strong-willed rancher whose name is now used to describe unorthodox individuals

Robert Mills 1781-1855, Charleston. Neo-classic architect

William Moultrie 1730-1805, Charleston. Revolutionary War general

Jim Rice, playing for the Boston Red Sox, was named to the American League All-Star team seven of his first ten seasons.

As a college student in 1963, Jesse Jackson lead a demonstration that ultimately led to the integration of Greensboro's restaurants and theaters.

William "Refrigerator" Perry b. 1962, Aiken. Football player

Joel Roberts Poinsett 1779-1851, Charleston. Diplomat

Joseph H. Rainey 1831-1887, Georgetown. The first black to serve in the U.S. House of Representatives

Willie Randolph b. 1954, Holly Hill. Baseball player

Jim Rice b. 1953, Anderson. Baseball player

Edward Rutledge 1749-1800, Charleston. Signer of the Declaration of Independence

Charles H. Townes b. 1915, Greenville. Nobel Prize-winning physicist; contributed to laser theory

William Travis 1809-1836, Red Banks. Officer in the Texas Revolution

Vanna White is the popular letter-turner on the television game show Wheel of Fortune.

Henry M. Turner 1834-1915, near Abbeville. Methodist bishop and the first black chaplain commissioned in the United States military forces

John B. Watson 1878-1958, Greenville. Psychologist

William Westmoreland b. 1914, Spartanburg County. Vietnam War general

Vanna White b. 1957, North Myrtle Beach. Television hostess

Cale Yarborough b. 1940 Greenville. Championship race car driver

Colleges and Universities
There are many colleges and universities in South Carolina. Here are the more prominent, with their locations, dates of founding, and enrollments.

Benedict College, Columbia, 1870, 1,207

Bob Jones University, Greenville, 1927, 4,390

The Citadel, The Military College of South Carolina,

Charleston, 1842, 3,600

Clemson University, Clemson, 1889, 17,666

College of Charleston, Charleston, 1770, 9,660

Columbia College, Columbia, 1854, 1,228

Converse College, Spartanburg, 1889, 1,120

Furman University, Greenville, 1825, 2,936

Lander College, Greenwood, 1872, 2,521

Limestone College, Gaffney, 1845, 860

Newberry College, Newberry, 1856, 711

Presbyterian College, Clinton, 1880, 1,167

South Carolina State College, Orangeburg, 1896, 5,024

University of South Carolina,

Columbia, 1801, 26,435; at Aiken, 1961, 3,208; at Spartanburg, 1967, 3,536

Winthrop College, Rock Hill, 1886, 5,025

Wofford College, Spartanburg, 1854, 1,127

Historic Tillman Hall serves as a landmark for Clemson University, a land-grant university with a threefold mission: teaching, research, and public service.

Where To Get More Information

Chamber of Commerce
930 Richland St., PO Box 1360
Columbia, SC 29201, or

So. Carolina Dept. of Parks, Recreation and Tourism
(803) 734-0122, or

Greater Columbia
Convention &
Visitor's Bureau
301 Gervais St.
Columbia, SC 29201
(803) 254-0479,

or call 1-800-346-3634

Further Reading

General

Aylesworth, Thomas G. and Virginia L. *State Reports: Lower Atlantic*. New York: Chelsea House, 1991.

North Carolina

Ashe, Samuel A. *History of North Carolina*. 2 vols. Spartanburg: Reprint Company, 1971.

Bell, Thelma H. and Corydon. *North Carolina*. New York: Coward, 1971.

Carpenter, Allan. *North Carolina*, rev. ed. Chicago: Children's Press, 1979.

Fradin, Dennis B. *From Sea to Shining Sea: South Carolina*. Chicago: Childrens Press, 1992.

Kent, Deborah. *America the Beautiful: South Carolina*. Chicago: Childrens Press, 1990.

Lefler, Hugh T., and Albert R. Newsome. *North Carolina*, rev. ed. Chapel Hill: University of North Carolina Press, 1963.

Lefler, Hugh T., and Albert R. Newsome. *North Carolina: The History of a Southern State*. 3rd ed. Chapel Hill: University of North Carolina Press, 1973.

Powell, William S. *The North Carolina Gazetteer*. Chapel Hill: University of North Carolina Press, 1968.

Powell, William S. *North Carolina: A Bicentennial History*. New York: Norton, 1977.

Powell, William S. *North Carolina, A History*. Nashville: American Association for State and Local History, 1985.

Roberts, Nancy. *The Goodliest Land: North Carolina*. New York: Doubleday, 1973.

Stein, R. Conrad. *America the Beautiful: North Carolina*. Chicago: Childrens Press, 1990.

South Carolina

Carpenter, Allan. *South Carolina*, rev. ed. Chicago: Childrens Press, 1979.

Fraden, Dennis B. *South Carolina in Words and Pictures*. Chicago: Children's Press, 1980.

Fradin, Dennis B. *From Sea to Shining Sea: North Carolina*. Chicago: Childrens Press, 1992.

Lander, Ernest, M. *A History of South Carolina, 1865-1960*. Columbia: University of South Carolina Press, 1970.

McCrady, Edward. *The History of South Carolina*. 4 vols. New York: Paladin Press, 1969.

Roberts, Bruce. *The Faces of South Carolina*. New York: Doubleday, 1976.

Sloan, Eugene B. *South Carolina: A Journalist and His State*. Columbia: Lewis-Sloan Publishing Comany, 1974.

Wallace, David D. *South Carolina, A Short History, 1520-1948*. Columbia: University of South Carolina Press, 1966.

Wright, Louis B. *South Carolina: A Bicentennial History*. New York: Norton, 1976.

Picture Credits